Sharks
Activity Book

Written by Catrin Morris

Song lyrics on page 16 written by Pippa Mayfield

Illustrated by Daniel Howarth

 Singing *    Reading    Speaking    Critical thinking

 Spelling    Writing    Listening *

* To complete these activities, listen to tracks 2, 3, and 4 of the audio download available at **www.ladybird.com/ladybirdreaders**

1 Match the words to the pictures.

1 basking shark

2 dwarf lantern shark

3 great white shark

4 hammerhead shark

5 mako shark

a
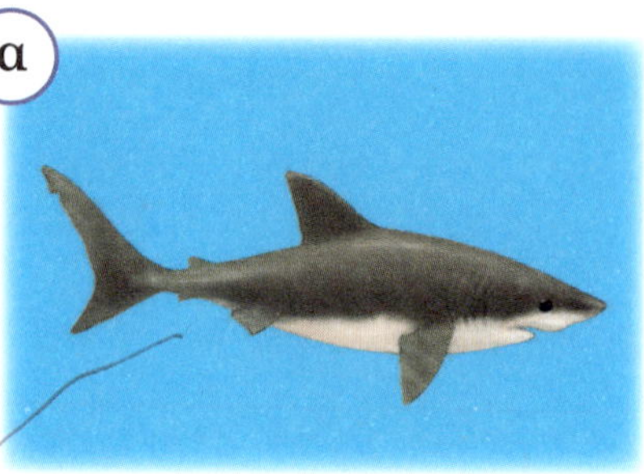

b
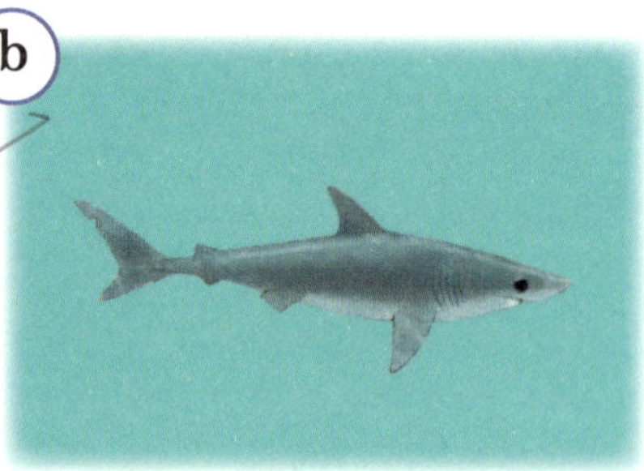

c
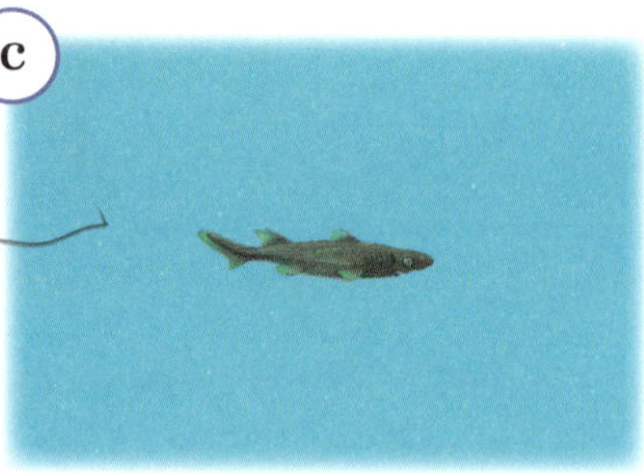

d
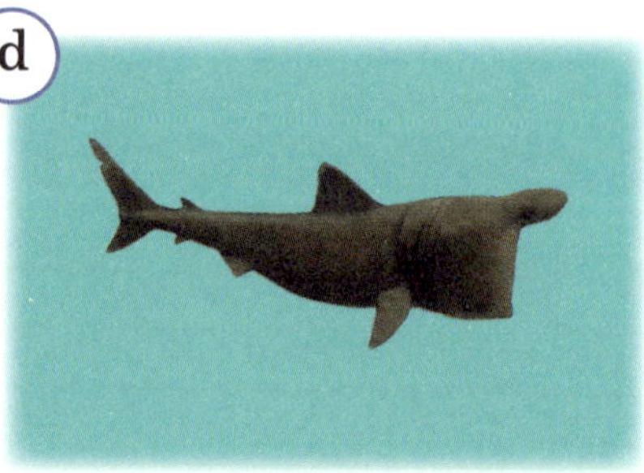

e
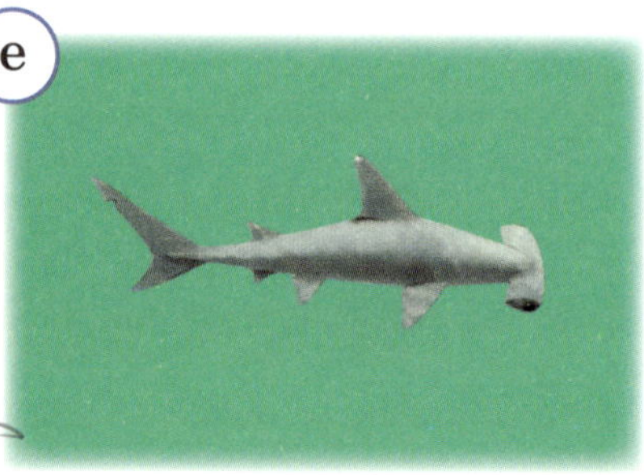

2 Look at the pictures and write the words from the box below.

| big | fast | light | little | teeth |

1  This is a __big__ shark.

2  This is a __little__ shark.

3  This is a __fast__ shark.

4  This shark has got big __teeth__.

5  This is a __light__-in-the-dark shark.

 **Listen and put a tick ✓ in the correct box.** *

1 Which is the boy's favorite shark?

a    b    c  ✓

2 What is the shark doing?

a    b    c

3 How old is the shark?

a    b    c

4 Which part of this shark's body is the girl talking about?

a    b    c

5 What is this shark good at?

a    b    c

4 Look and read. Write the answer using *What, Why, When,* or *Where.*

1 __What__ kind of shark is this?
It's a hammerhead shark.

2 __Where__ does it live?
In the sea.

3 __Why__ has it got a long head?
To help it catch food.

4 __What__ does it do with its head?
It holds fish and eats them.

5 __When__ does it swim?
It swims all the time.

5 Look at the pictures. Put a ✓ by the correct word.

1 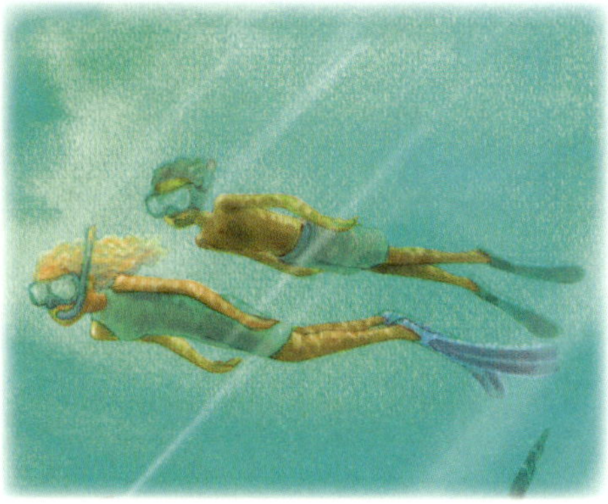
a swim ✓
b swimm ☐

2 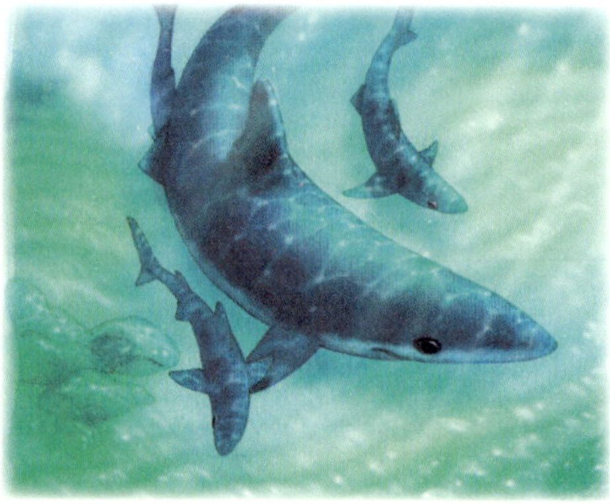
a paps ☐
b pups ✓

3 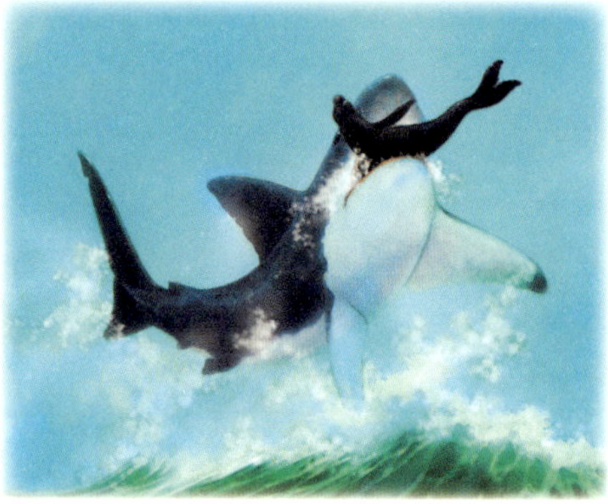
a cach ☐
b catch ✓

4 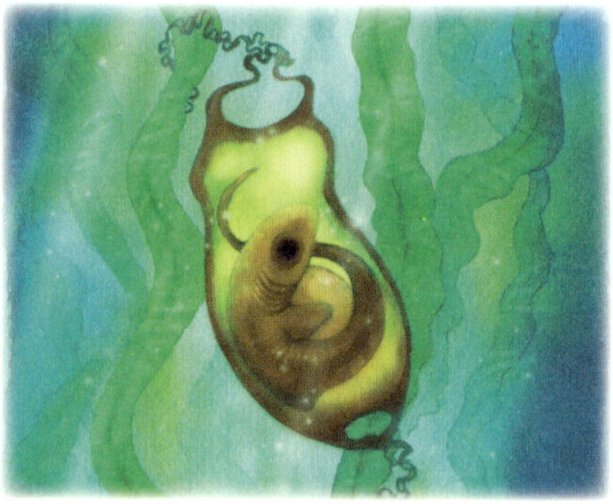
a eg ☐
b egg ✓

5 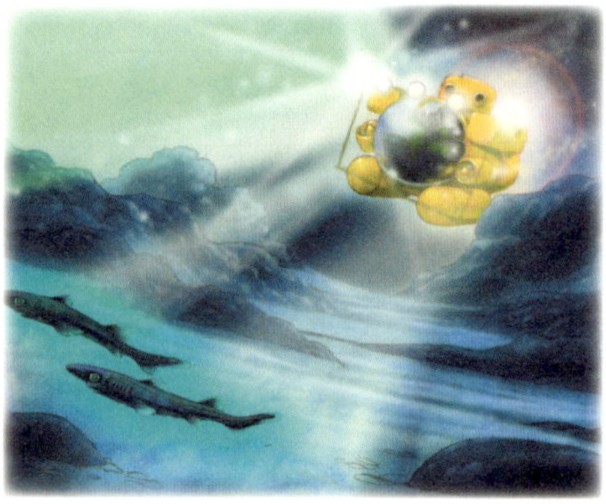
a light ✓
b lyte ☐

6 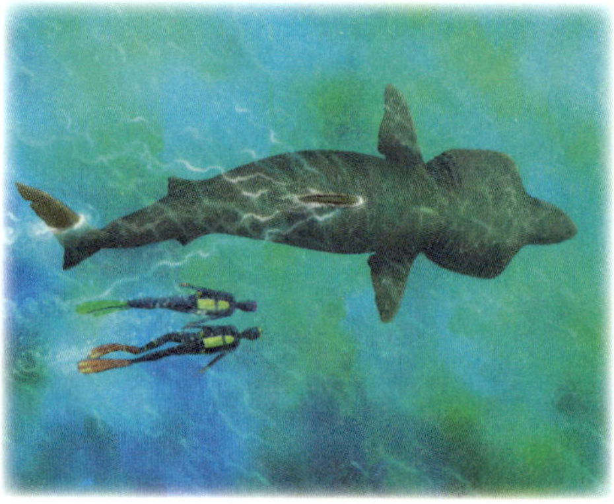
a bis ☐
b big ✓

6 Choose the correct words and write them on the lines below.

pups

head

plankton

teeth

sea animal

egg

Sharks use these to catch food:

teeth, head

Sharks eat these:

sea animal, egg, plankton

Sharks are these before they grow big:

egg, pups

7 Listen and write.  *

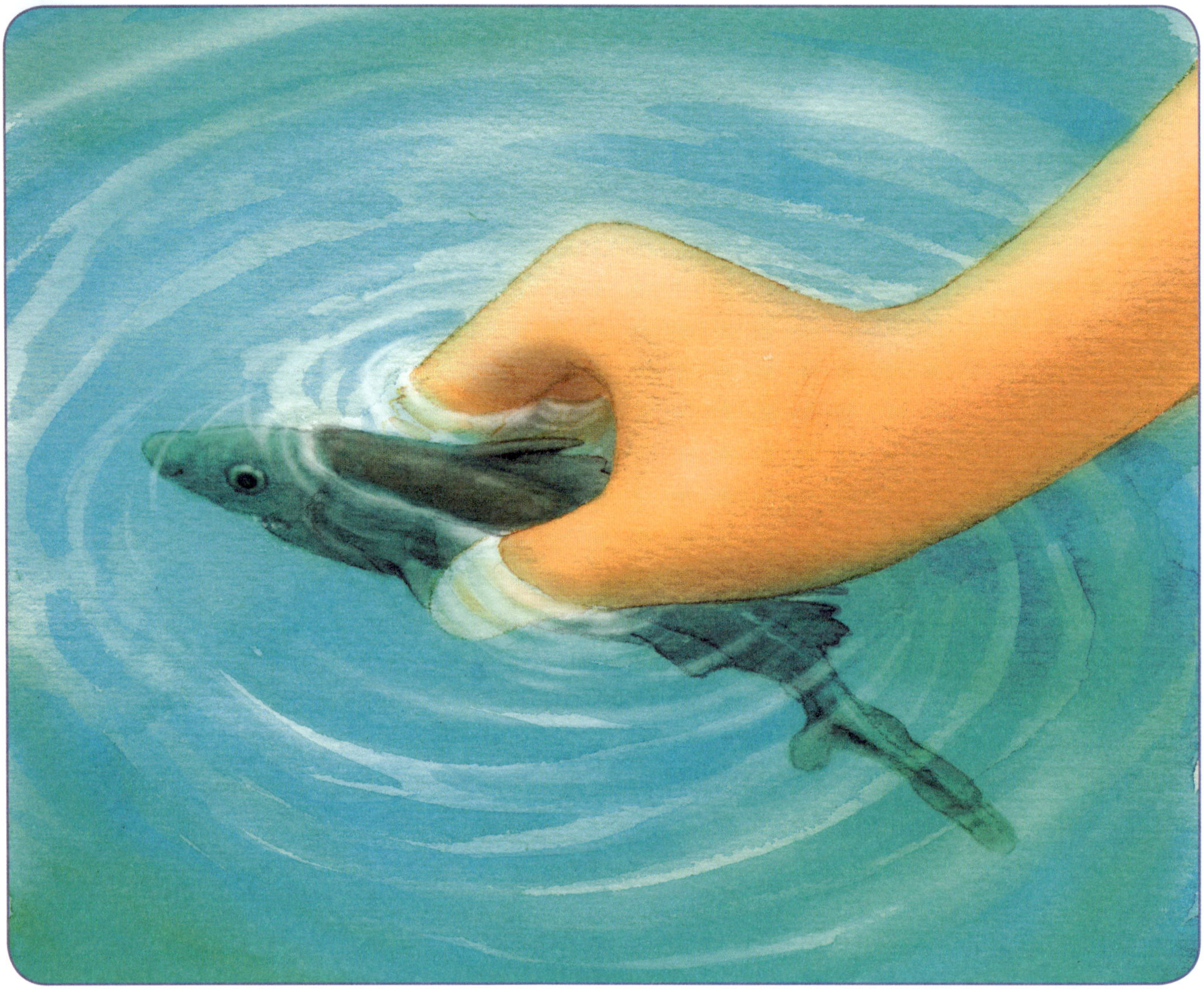

1 What's the name of the shark? dwarf lantern shark

2 Is it a big shark? No, it's smaller than a ....

3 Where does it live? In the sea, ... America.

4 What does it eat? Small ....

5 What color is it? .... and black.

6 What can it do? Make a .... with its body.

8 Work with a friend. Look at the pictures. Ask and answer questions about the sharks.

1 Is this is a small shark?

Yes. It's called a dwarf lantern shark.

2 What color is this shark?

3 What does this shark eat?

4 Can this shark swim fast?

 **Look and read. Put a ✓ by the correct picture.**

1 People are frightened of this shark.

 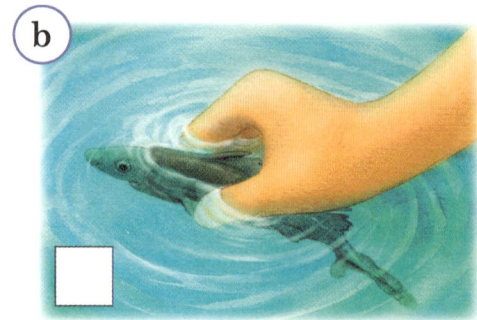

2 Which shark has big teeth?

3 Which shark grows inside its mother?

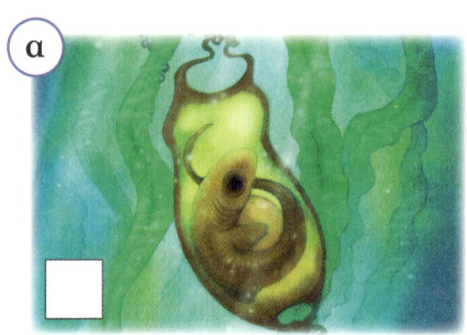 

4 Which shark makes a light?

10 Read and write *and*, *because*, or *but*.

1 Great white sharks catch fish __because__ they swim very fast.

2 A shark loses its teeth, __but__ it grows new ones.

3 Basking sharks don't eat other fish __because__ they don't have big teeth.

4 Some shark pups have to find food __because__ their mothers don't help them.

5 A great white shark swam to Australia __and__ back again to Africa!

6 Many sharks don't come from eggs __but__ they grow inside their mothers.

11 Look at the pictures. Match the two parts of the words.

1. bask — ing shark
2. hammer — head shark
3. plank — ton
4. dwarf — lantern shark
5. mako — shark
6. great — white shark

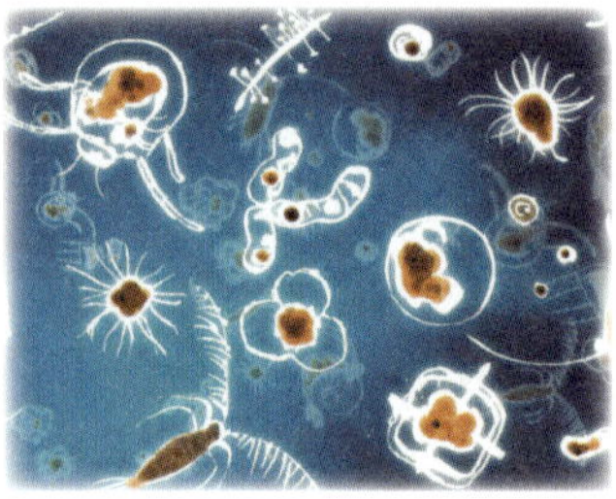

Look at the picture and read the story. Write some words to complete the sentences.

Hello, I'm a mako shark pup. I didn't come from an egg. I grew inside my mother. Now, I live with my mother and brother. But, I have to find and eat fish. My mother doesn't help me do this.

1 She is a ……… mako ……… shark pup.

2 Mako pups don't come from ……… an egg ……… .

3 They grow inside their ……… mother ……… .

4 They have to find and eat ……… fish ……… .

5 Their mothers don't ……… help ……… them.

13 Work with a friend. Ask and answer questions about sharks.

1 Do you like sharks?

Yes, I do.

2 What are sharks good at?

3 Why are people frightened of sharks?

4 Are you frightened of any animals?

14 Read and circle the correct verbs.

1 Great white sharks' bodies **help / helps** them to go fast.

2 Great white sharks often **see / sees** a fish that they **want / wants** to eat.

3 Then, they **swim / swims** very fast to catch it and eat it.

4 Sometimes, a shark **lose / loses** its teeth, but it **grow / grows** new ones.

15 Sing the song. *

A little fish said, "I'm afraid of sharks!
Great whites and hammerheads are bigger than me!"
I told the fish, "And they're faster, too!
But there are lots of different sharks in the sea.

Do not be afraid! That's a basking shark!
It is very, very big. But what does it eat?
Lots and lots of plankton, which are very, very small.
There are lots of different sharks in the sea.

Do not be afraid! That's a dwarf lantern shark.
It is very, very small. And look, can you see?
A light in the water that its body makes.
There are lots of different sharks swimming in the sea."

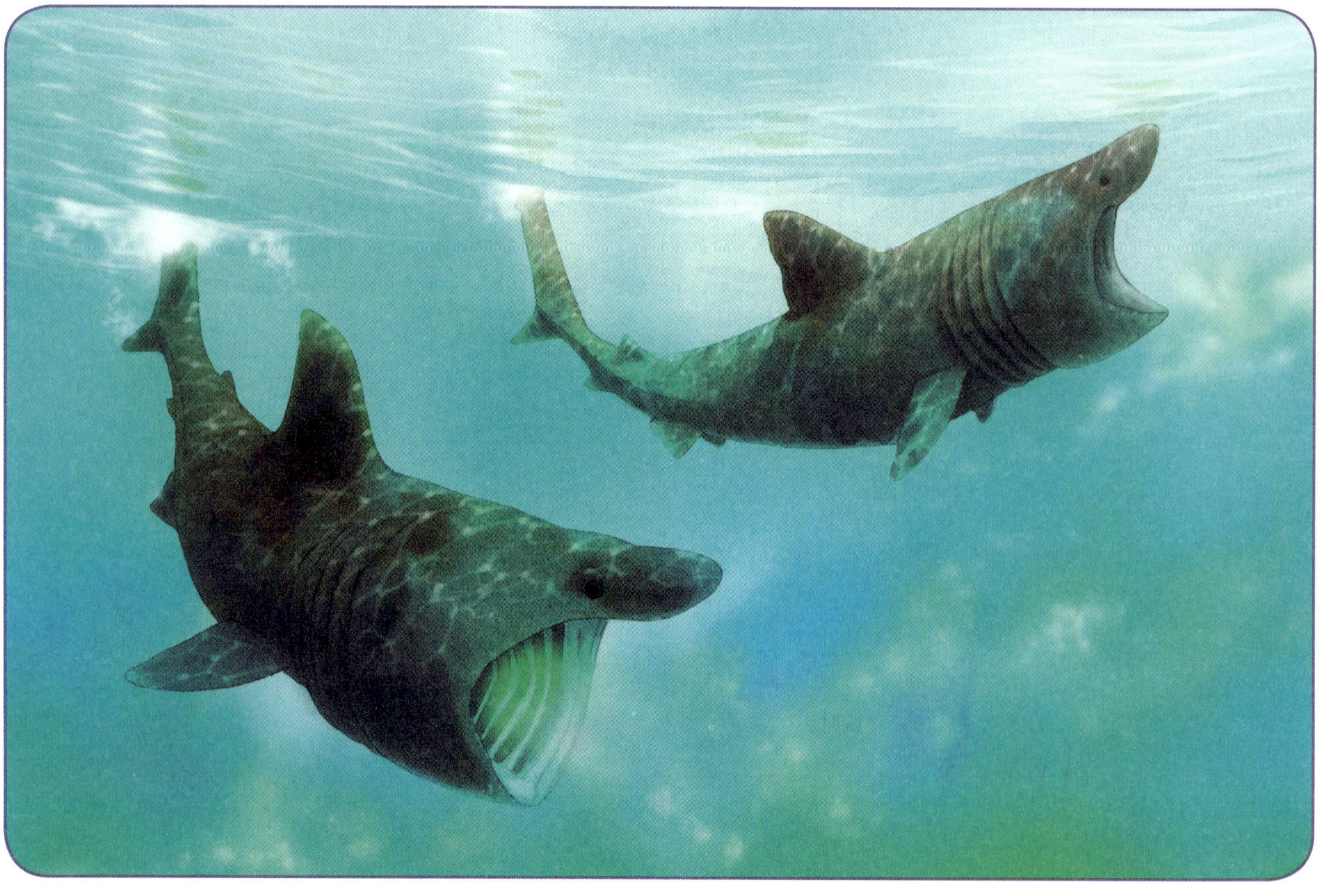

* To complete this activity, listen to track 4 of the audio download available at **www.ladybird.com/ladybirdreaders**